F FOU

Greater Than a Tourist Book Series
Reviews from Readers

I think the series is wonderful and beneficial for tourists to get information before visiting the city.

-Seckin Zumbul, Izmir Turkey

I am a world traveler who has read many trip guides but this one really made a difference for me. I would call it a heartfelt creation of a local guide expert instead of just a guide.

-Susy, Isla Holbox, Mexico

New to the area like me, this is a must have!

-Joe, Bloomington, USA

This is a good series that gets down to it when looking for things to do at your destination without having to read a novel for just a few ideas.

-Rachel, Monterey, USA

Good information to have to plan my trip to this destination.

-Pennie Farrell, Mexico

Great ideas for a port day.

-Mary Martin USA

Aptly titled, you won't just be a tourist after reading this book. You'll be greater than a tourist!

-Alan Warner, Grand Rapids, USA

Even though I only have three days to spend in San Miguel in an upcoming visit, I will use the author's suggestions to guide some of my time there. An easy read - with chapters named to guide me in directions I want to go.

 -Robert Catapano, USA

Great insights from a local perspective! Useful information and a very good value!

 -Sarah, USA

This series provides an in-depth experience through the eyes of a local. Reading these series will help you to travel the city in with confidence and it'll make your journey a unique one.

-Andrew Teoh, Ipoh, Malaysia

>TOURIST

GREATER THAN A TOURIST- COSTA RICA

50 Travel Tips from a Local

Jonathan El-aziz

Greater Than a Tourist- Copyright © 2019 by CZYK Publishing LLC. All Rights Reserved.

All rights reserved. No part of this book may be reproduced in any form or by any electronic or mechanical means including information storage and retrieval systems, without permission in writing from the author. The only exception is by a reviewer, who may quote short excerpts in a review.

The statements in this book are of the authors and may not be the views of CZYK Publishing or Greater Than a Tourist.

Cover designed by: Ivana Stamenkovic
Cover Image: https://pixabay.com/photos/costa-rica-plant-beach-palm-4018153/

CZYK Publishing Since 2011.

Greater Than a Tourist
Visit our website at GreaterThanaTourist.com

Lock Haven, PA
All rights reserved.

ISBN: 9781095176863

… # >TOURIST

50 TRAVEL TIPS FROM A LOCAL

\>TOURIST

BOOK DESCRIPTION

Are you excited about planning your next trip?

Do you want to try something new?

Would you like some guidance from a local?

If you answered yes to any of these questions, then this Greater Than a Tourist book is for you.

Greater Than a Tourist- Costa Rica by Jonathan El-aziz gives you the inside scoop on Costa Rica. Most travel books tell you how to travel like a tourist. Although there is nothing wrong with that, as part of the Greater Than a Tourist series, this book will give you travel tips from someone who has lived at your next travel destination.

In these pages, you will discover advice that will help you throughout your stay. This book will not tell you exact addresses or store hours but instead will give you excitement and knowledge from a local that you may not find in other smaller print travel books.

Travel like a local. Slow down, stay in one place, and get to know the people and culture. By the time you finish this book, you will be eager and prepared to travel to your next destination.

Inside this travel guide book you will find:

- Insider tips from a local.
- Bonus tips *50 Things to Know About Packing Light for Travel* by bestselling author Manidipa Bhattacharyya.
- Packing and planning list.
- List of travel questions to ask yourself or others while traveling.
- A place to write your travel bucket list.

OUR STORY

Traveling is a passion of the "Greater than a Tourist" series creator. Lisa studied abroad in college, and for their honeymoon Lisa and her husband toured Europe. During her travels to Malta, an older man tried to give her some advice based on his own experience living on the island since he was a young boy. She was not sure if she should talk to the stranger but was interested in his advice. When traveling to some places she was wary to talk to locals because she was afraid that they weren't being genuine. Through her travels, Lisa learned how much locals had to share with tourists. Lisa created the *Greater Than a Tourist* book series to help connect people with locals. A topic that locals are very passionate about sharing.

>TOURIST

TABLE OF CONTENTS

BOOK DESCRIPTION
Our Story
TABLE OF CONTENTS
DEDICATION
ABOUT THE AUTHOR
HOW TO USE THIS BOOK
FROM THE PUBLISHER
WELCOME TO
> TOURIST
Tips to take in count to have a grateful journey in Costa Rica
1. Costa Rica is not cheap as neighborhood countries
2. it's a small country but it takes longer than it seems to get around
3. Tap water is safe to drink
4. Dengue, not malaria, is the main disease from mosquitoes in Costa Rica
5. It gets cold but it doesn't snow
6. US dollars are readily accepted and are the standard currency in tourism
7. Rainy season doesn't mean it's bad to travel
8. Sloths aren't everywhere (sorry)
9. Police can stop and ask for your papers at any time

10. Wi-Fi is readily available…
11. Not every town has an ATM
12. Despite the laid back attitude of Ticos, they drive very crazy
13. San Jose's not as bad as people make it out to be…
14. English language is widely spoken but not all Costa Ricans speak English
15. Locals love to talk to foreigners
16. Costa Rica doesn't have much in common with Mexico
17. Costa Rica is very safe and theft is the most common crime

5o Travel Tips to do in Costa Rica
1. Go horseback riding
2. Ziplining
3. Sunset Sailing Cruise
4. Snorkeling or Scuba Diving
5. Private Boating Tour in Gulf of Papagayo
6. Get a Massage on the Beach
7. Surfing
8. Canyoning
9. Beach Hop
10. Eat a Copo (or a Churchill in Puntarenas)
11. Visit the Fiestas Civicas
12. Isla Tortuga Cruise

>TOURIST

13. Road Trip the Central Valley
14. Combination Adventure Tour in Rincon de la Vieja
15. Waterslide in the Middle of the Jungle
16. Visit Finca to See the Stone Spheres
17. Stand Up Paddle Board in the Ocean
18. Visit Catarata Llanos de Cortes
19. Visit Catarata del Toro
20. See Turtles at Ostional Wildlife Refuge
21. Visit the Jaguar Rescue Center in Puerto Viejo
22. Go Fishing
23. Walk Through San Jose
24. Kayak Tortuguero National Park
25. Explore Arenal Volcano National Park
26. Ride a Tram Through the Rainforest
27. White Water Raft Rio Pacuare
28. Go on a Waterfall Tour
29. See Monkeys and Sloths at Manuel Antonio National Park
30. Visit a Volcano
31. Explore Caves at Barra Honda National Park
32. See Rio Celeste
33. Wildlife Watching Safari Float
34. Go on a Coffee Tour
35. See the Crocodiles at Rio Tarcoles
36. Go on a Chocolate Tour

37. See the Whale's Tail at Marino Ballena National Park
38. Eat a Chifrijo
39. Eat Rice and Beans
40. Enjoy the Hot Springs in Arenal
41. Go Whale Watching
42. Get a Pipa Fria
43. Go Bird Watching
44. Play with Puppies at Territorio de Zaguates
45. Go on a Night Walk
46. Watch a Futbol Game at the National Stadium in La Sabana
47. Try Costa Rican Local and Craft Beer
48. Hike Corcovado National Park
49. Walk the Hanging Bridges in the Monteverde Cloud Forests
50. Enjoy the Pura Vida Life!

50 THINGS TO KNOW ABOUT PACKING LIGHT FOR TRAVEL

Packing and Planning Tips

Travel Questions

Travel Bucket List

>TOURIST

DEDICATION

To My Family:

I though you never were going to believe on my freelance job until I did my first freelance job and get my first payment. That was a very exciting moment and you celebrated it with me joyfully, I am so thankful to you for supporting me and cheering on me to go on and never give up, so, I ask to God for a big blessing on you for everything you did for me and may our familiar union keep strong forever.

Yours, Jonathan El-aziz.

ABOUT THE AUTHOR

Jonathan El-aziz is a costa rican native who lives in Cortés, a small city/town of the province of Puntarenas, loves to help visitors to be noticed about everything about the zone.

Jonathan El-aziz loves to travel within the country and meet humble people to share knowledge about the zone he visits, -"I like meeting places I never visited, although I know practically the majority of places my parents lived in when I was a baby"- points El-aziz, "The people of every place you visit, has its own habits and life customs as well as their speaking accent that you will notice clearly when you speak with them, take costa rican spanish classes"-smiles-.

With all this we say good bye to Jonathan El-aziz, and we hope this book help you to enjoy your journey in Costa Rica.

>TOURIST

HOW TO USE THIS BOOK

The *Greater Than a Tourist* book series was written by someone who has lived in an area for over three months. The goal of this book is to help travelers either dream or experience different locations by providing opinions from a local. The author has made suggestions based on their own experiences. Please check before traveling to the area in case the suggested places are unavailable.

Travel Advisories: As a first step in planning any trip abroad, check the Travel Advisories for your intended destination.
https://travel.state.gov/content/travel/en/traveladvisories/traveladvisories.html

FROM THE PUBLISHER

Traveling can be one of the most important parts of a person's life. The anticipation and memories that you have are some of the best. As a publisher of the Greater Than a Tourist book series, as well as the popular *50 Things to Know* book series, we strive to help you learn about new places, spark your imagination, and inspire you. Wherever you are and whatever you do I wish you safe, fun, and inspiring travel.

Lisa Rusczyk Ed. D.
CZYK Publishing

>TOURIST

WELCOME TO
> TOURIST

>TOURIST

"Man cannot discover new oceans unless he has the courage to lose sight of the shore"

-Andre Gide.

Do you have an icon that inspire you to travel such as a whale tail, a wood picture, a bird or a beach picture? It can be a nice inspiring icon that may make good vibes to make a great adventure.

It's no longer a life time's dream: the beach and the lush vegetation, the warm climate, cool nights, good food, kind people, a great community and far from the traffic of the big cites because it becomes reality: A more relaxed lifestyle.

Yet my life in the south pacific of Costa Rica has turned out to be very active, apart from traveling through the country, interviewing local people for more tips and photo shooting for my remembrances it became my preferred endeavors. Travelers today are turning increasingly towards the planet as an exciting adventurous and exotic destination. Of the many attractive tropical countries to choose, Costa Rica stands out as the most delightful in the world. There are not only tropical rainforests and beautiful beaches but also nice surprises: Active volcanoes and windswept mountaintops, so although Costa Rica is a small country, a large variety of tropical habitats are found within it –and they are protected by the best developed conservation programme in Latin America-that makes Costa Rica famous for its enlightened approach to conservation.

More than a quarter of the country land in Costa Rica is protected by the potential explanation of national parks, wild life refuges, marine sanctuaries, national reserves, conservation areas and biological reserves. It's estimated that approximately the 25% of the areas -both private and public- is part of the national park system and spherical conservation. Green tropical rainforest, mangroves cloud forests, spectaculars beaches, volcanoes, waterfalls and coral reefs are just some of many habitats protected by national parks and reserves of

Costa Rica; these national parks and conservation areas offer a wealth of diversity for visitors. Costa Rica supplies around 58 wild life refuges, 32 protected areas, 27 national parks, 15 wet lands, 11 rain forests and 8 biological reserves dedicated to the country's natural

diversity. More than 35.000 species of insects, an estimated of 220 species of a reptiles and160 species of amphibians can be found in this tropical paradise.

>TOURIST

Not only safe but friendly, costarricans delights in showing off their lovely country manners to treat visitors, you will hear the common phrase of "Pura vida!" when they greet you (it's pronounced 'poura vida' and means "pure life", a sign of plenty life) and wherever you go, you will find the locals to be in constant source of help, smiles, and information. The transportation system it's a little expensive and covers the whole country, so Costa Rica is at same time one of the most beautiful and one of the easiest tropical counties to travel in. This book will help you with a place at once of every Costa Rica's province(state), with some tips to take in mind wherever you go through the seven provinces of Costa Rica, no matter what you budget.

>TOURIST

TIPS TO TAKE IN COUNT TO HAVE A GRATEFUL JOURNEY IN COSTA RICA

1. COSTA RICA IS NOT CHEAP AS NEIGHBORHOOD COUNTRIES

This is one of the most important things to know about Costa Rica. Many people assume that Central America automatically equals cheap travel. Nope!. That is the biggest misconception about Costa Rica. But really it's northern neighbor, Nicaragua and is dirt cheap but it's is also one of the poorest countries in the world so you can stretch your money very far there.

It's no wonder tourists who didn't research properly get a nasty surprised when they find out tours can easily cost $100, food is the same price as North America and gas is nearly twice as much as the US. Without careful planning and budgeting, you can blow through hundreds of dollars fairly quickly.

2. IT'S A SMALL COUNTRY BUT IT TAKES LONGER THAN IT SEEMS TO GET AROUND

Costa Rica is a little smaller than West Virginia so it's easy to think you can road trip the whole country in a week. Technically you can, but trust me, that wouldn't be very fun!

This is because the roads in Costa Rica are never as the crows fly. They do have highways and the main roads are paved but they usually have only one lane. Unfortunately, all the big trailer trucks have to drive on the same roads causing a lot of traffic and congestion.

For example, Tamarindo to San Jose is 259 kilometers or 161 miles and it takes us 4-5 hours driving on average. Many people when planning their itinerary try to stuff as many places as possible but think about it. Do you really want to be driving 3-5 hours every 2 days and not have enough time to truly get to know a place?

This is one of the mistakes to avoid when traveling in Costa Rica. Don't try to drive everywhere in a short trip. In Costa Rica, it's best to take it slow and enjoy the scenery! For a one week trip it's best to choose 2 destinations or pick a home base and do day trips.

3. TAP WATER IS SAFE TO DRINK

In the cities and most touristic destinations, you can indeed drink the tap water. Hotels will indicate whether the water is safe and tour guides will let you know which faucets to use.

Though tap water is generally safe to drink (avoid drinking water in rural areas and always ask your hotel), I still recommend bringing a filter if you're sensitive. You can also help the environment by bringing an insulated water bottle.

4. DENGUE, NOT MALARIA, IS THE MAIN DISEASE FROM MOSQUITOES IN COSTA RICA

The mosquito borne disease travelers should concern themselves with in Costa Rica is Dengue Fever, not malaria. As it turns out, Costa Rica has been leading

Central America with the most reported cases of dengue. There were over 22,000 reported cases in 2016 but the lowest number of cases (5561) in 2017 and 373 in 2018 so far.

It's a huge misconception that Costa Rica is rampant with Malaria and Zika. In fact, Costa Rica has had a 90% reduction in Malaria cases between 2000 and 2010. As for Zika, there have been 2,000 cases in 2017, nearly all from local citizens, not tourists.

Extra travel safety tip: Make sure to purchase travel insurance just in case you do catch something!

5. IT GETS COLD BUT IT DOESN'T SNOW

Costa Rica experiences typical tropical weather but it has many micro-climates. It doesn't snow but it does get quite cold in some areas due to the elevation and the ecosystems. It gets chilly when you're up 3,000 meters in the clouds!

Some of the colder areas are Monteverde, Poas, San Isidro de Perez Zeledon and San Gerardo de Dota. Temperatures in those areas can get down to the 60's

>TOURIST

Fahrenheit at night. The coasts stay nice and hot, in the 80's and 90's.

Make sure to research the area you are visiting so you come prepared. For packing tips, check out our Costa Rica packing list to see what you need to bring for different activities and destinations.

6. US DOLLARS ARE READILY ACCEPTED AND ARE THE STANDARD CURRENCY IN TOURISM

Hotels and tour companies quote their prices in USD since majority of the tourists are US citizens. Additionally, Costa Ricans can have bank accounts in USD as mortgages and car payments are quoted in USD. US dollars have become the standard currency in tourism.

So when you're trying to get your money together, don't stress too much about exchanging it all beforehand as it's not 100% necessary. You can use dollars in pretty much every touristic destination and they will give you your change back in colones. If you are Canadian however, it will be better for you to have colones due to the Canadian dollar and USD exchange rate. But unfortunately, all the tourist services (tours, hotels) are in USD.

Make sure you check what the exchange rate is. Since the exchange rate is around 600 to 1, some places may try to stiff you by using a 500 to 1 rate and you will lose out a bit.

7. RAINY SEASON DOESN'T MEAN IT'S BAD TO TRAVEL

Summer or dry season in Costa Rica is our high tourism season because everyone wants to escape the winter up north and soak in the sun. On the other hand, rainy season is equally as wonderful but many people are scared to visit Costa Rica during this time even though it's really not that bad.

A typical rainy season day is sunny and hot in the morning, cloudy in the afternoon and rainy in the evening/night.

If you're not sure, here are 6 more reasons why you should visit Costa Rica in rainy season. In my experience, I love rainy season in Costa Rica. No crowds, more wildlife and it's cheaper!

>TOURIST

Costa Rica's rainy season is around beginning of May to end of November. The rainiest months for most of Costa Rica is September and October and November and July for the Caribbean. You do need to pack appropriately for rainy season. Don't get caught in a rainstorm unprepared!

8. SLOTHS AREN'T EVERYWHERE (SORRY)

As much as I hate to break it to you, sloths aren't everywhere. I know Costa Rica markets their cuddly sloths so much it seems that the roads are crawling with them but it's not true. Sloths, being the masters of camouflage, are very difficult to see without a guide or trained eye.

Sloths are found in almost all of Costa Rica but very hard to see in some places than others. For example, it is incredibly difficult to see one in Guanacaste due to the extremely dry climate. Head down to the humid South Pacific or the Caribbean and sloths are much more common.

One of the main "complaints" I've heard from visitors is that they didn't see a sloth. I asked them where they were in Costa Rica and many of them were at the Pacific coast beach where they don't live. If you really want to see a sloth, then you need to go to where they are more common. To make sure you see a sloth, hire a guide. They have trained eyes and normally have binoculars or telescopes to find them.

9. POLICE CAN STOP AND ASK FOR YOUR PAPERS AT ANY TIME

In Costa Rica, police are legally allowed to stop any car and ask for papers. Always have a color copy of your passport and photo of your tourist stamp with you. Remember that to legally drive in Costa Rica as a tourist, you need to have your original passport (not a color copy), your original driver's license and a valid tourist stamp with you.

If a police stops you, they'll ask you for your passport, ask you where you're going and then send you on your way. Most of the time they don't ask anything else and many of them speak a degree of English.

>TOURIST

Also something else to note is that the police in Costa Rica are very nice and there is a sector specifically for tourists. They hand out safety tips and maps to tourists and are happy to answer questions.

10. WI-FI IS READILY AVAILABLE...

...at hotels. It is common for hotels to offer free Wi-Fi and many of them have it available throughout the whole property. Some hotels may only have it in reception but it is free.

However, it's hard to find open Wi-Fi in public places. It's not like NYC where you can find a Starbucks and use the free Wi-Fi. If you see a restaurant with a secure Wi-Fi connection, you can ask them for the password as a customer. I've found most places are OK with giving it out.

If you always want Internet during your time in Costa Rica, we highly recommend getting a prepaid sim card for your phone in an I.C.E agency(Costar Rican Electricity Institute)

11. NOT EVERY TOWN HAS AN ATM

If you're planning a very off the beaten path trip to Costa Rica, do note that some places don't have an ATM. All touristic destinations such as Arenal, Monteverde, Puerto Viejo and Tamarindo do, but towns like Drake Bay do not. Make sure you bring enough cash (and colones is best).

12. DESPITE THE LAID BACK ATTITUDE OF TICOS, THEY DRIVE VERY CRAZY

People are always surprised by the driving in Costa Rica and it's something I warn people about when they are renting a car in Costa Rica.
One of my friends was so taken aback that she asked me why the driving is so crazy if Ticos are so pura vida? I told her that it's probably because they are always late to everything (aka Tico Time) so they have to drive super-fast! It is a bit shocking when Costa Ricans, who are generally relaxed, happy go

> TOURIST

lucky people completely change when they get behind the wheel.
Simply stated, if you're not used to this kind of driving, be very careful and always drive defensively. Ticos will cut you off, tailgate, never use their blinker, jump the line and ignore red lights. Most of that type of driving is in San Jose however. Once you get out to the rural areas, it's much more relaxed.

13. SAN JOSE'S NOT AS BAD AS PEOPLE MAKE IT OUT TO BE...

...for a few days. I'll be honest, we don't really like San Jose. It's dirty, crowded and not aesthetically pleasing. However, the capital city does have some hidden gems and all it takes is a day or two to get to know San Jose. You can find some of the best restaurants and craft beer in San Jose!
Then there are the cultural gems: the National Theater and museums. Any history lover will want to stop by the city as there are few museums of this quality anywhere else in the country.
San Jose really isn't as bad as people make it out to be for 1 or 2 days. And honestly, it is the best place to

experience Costa Rican life since over 1 million Ticos live and work in the capital city (out of a population of 5 million).

14. ENGLISH LANGUAGE IS WIDELY SPOKEN BUT NOT ALL COSTA RICANS SPEAK ENGLISH

People assume that because Costa Rica is a touristic country and that there are so many North Americans here, that all the locals know English. Though many Costa Ricans know a degree of English, not all of them do. These are mostly the Ticos that live in the city or work in tourism since English is required for jobs.

The bottom line is don't assume that you can speak English to everyone. It'll be helpful to learn a bit of Spanish, at least the basic words.

>TOURIST

15. LOCALS LOVE TO TALK TO FOREIGNERS

And I mean, they'll stop you on the street to talk to you. They're very gregarious people with a curious nature and since tourism in Costa Rica is on the rise, they enjoy meeting people from all walks of life.

A word of caution to solo female travelers: Tico men are very forward and quite assertive when they see a single female walking by herself, they have no reservations to ask you if you have a boyfriend or who you're in Costa Rica with and it might take a bit of effort to get them to go away. My advice is to smile politely and move on if you don't want to talk to them.

Advice for families with babies: Ticos also love babies. They will stop you on the street, pick them up, hold and kiss them without asking. If you don't feel comfortable with this, politely say No tocar por favor! (Don't touch please!).

16. COSTA RICA DOESN'T HAVE MUCH IN COMMON WITH MEXICO

Costa Rica receives most of their tourists from the United States and for some reason, many North Americans think Costa Rica is like Mexico. But Costa Rica and Mexico are completely different!
Costa Rican food isn't like Mexican food at all and even the Spanish spoken in both countries aren't the same. In Costa Rica, they don't say andale or anything like that. Think about it, even the locations are different. Costa Rica is in Central America and Mexico is in North America. They are two very different countries.

17. COSTA RICA IS VERY SAFE AND THEFT IS THE MOST COMMON CRIME

Did you know that Costa Rica is one of 23 countries in the world with no military? There is only the police force, the OIJ and GAO (swat).

>TOURIST

Costa Rica is a very safe country in Latin America for traveling, especially families.

The most common crime in Costa Rica is theft: car/house break ins and pick pockets. Many times it is because tourists left their belongings on the beach and went swimming. They come back to find their belongings gone. Or they don't lock the car door or leave the windows open.

So when you're traveling in Costa Rica, make sure to always lock the door, roll up the windows, have one person stay with your stuff at all times and don't leave any valuables visible in the car.

If you prefer a tourist guide to take you around any city you visit, look for information at the hotel's reception and if you travel by bus take care of your luggage and pick your documents and money on a handbag.

50 TRAVEL TIPS TO DO IN COSTA RICA

1. GO HORSEBACK RIDING

Horseback riding is a common activity in Costa Rica to do at the beach or the mountains. It's a fun way to see the Costa Rican landscapes and scenery and is a great group activity.

Horseback riding in Rincon de la Vieja National Park

You can horseback ride in nearly every touristic destination in the country and it's one of the best things to do in Guanacaste where there are a handful of haciendas (farms). Many of the local farmers rent out their horses for tours and costs anywhere from $35 -55 depending on how long the tour is and where it takes you. Several beach towns like Samara, Monteuma and Tamarindo offer horseback riding tours on the beach.

>TOURIST

2. ZIPLINING

Ziplining is one of the essential things to do in Costa Rica (read why every traveler should go ziplining in Costa Rica). You really can't visit Costa Rica and not zipline since they are world famous for their long cables with spectacular views.

If you're scared of heights, don't worry. Ziplining in Costa Rica doesn't automatically mean every one is the highest or tallest. There are beginner to intermediate canopy tours like Athica in Arenal, Hacienda Roble near Tamarindo, Congo Canopy Tour in Gulf of Papagayo and Wingnuts in Samara.

For the thrill seeker, they will love the extreme ziplining at 100% Aventura in Monteverde, Sky Adventures in Monteverde and Arenal or the new Diamante Adventures in Guanacaste (get 10% off here) with the longest ocean view zipline!

Canopy tours cost from $35 to $75 depending on if you need transportation. If there is any one adventure activity to do in Costa Rica, it is ziplining! It is one of the most popular things to do in Costa Rica!

3. SUNSET SAILING CRUISE

This is one of the most relaxing and romantic things to do in Costa Rica: go on a sunset cruise and it's particularly popular in Guanacaste because of the beautiful beaches up and down the Pacific coast. You can also go in Manuel Antonio and Playa Herradura/Jaco.

Nearly every beach town on the Pacific Coast like Playas del Coco, Playa Flamingo and Playa Tamarindo offers sunset cruises as a way to experience the ocean. Most offer snorkeling, drinks and snacks and there is a good chance to see marine wildlife.

Sunset sailing cruises run from around $70-85 per person and usually include snorkel equipment, fruit, water, drinks and snacks. It's a super romantic activity in Costa Rica as you sail under a beautiful sunset, cuddling up with your loved one.

>TOURIST

4. SNORKELING OR SCUBA DIVING

Snorkeling is a must-do activity in Costa Rica and the best places are the Gulf of Papagayo, Caribbean (during certain times of the year) and Isla del Caño.

Scuba diving is also excellent in Costa Rica and popular dive sites are Bat Islands, Catalina Islands and Cano Island.

For those who want experience the best dive site, head to Cocos Island, a World Heritage Site that houses huge populations of hammerhead sharks, giana mantas, yellowfin tuna and more. It takes a couple days on a boat to get there and it's fairly expensive so it's definitely one for the world bucket list.

A 2 tank dive costs roughly $115 and the best towns to stay at for scuba diving are Playa Flamingo, Playas del Coco, Uvita, Playa Ocotal and Playa Tamarindo. You can also scuba dive in Manuel Antonio, Cahuita and Drake Bay.

5. PRIVATE BOATING TOUR IN GULF OF PAPAGAYO

Boating is the best way to see islands and hidden beaches in Guanacaste and it's one of our favorite things to do in Costa Rica when we have friends or family in town.

Private boating tours allow you to go to however many beaches you want, stay as long as you want and make your own schedule as opposed to an open/public tour which is always on a set schedule.One of our friends has a boating company in Playas del Coco and we love going on private boating tours with him since he knows the best snorkel spots and we always have the beach all to ourselves!

6. GET A MASSAGE ON THE BEACH

What is more relaxing than getting a massage on the beach? Not much! You can find many massage stands on the beach and it's not too expensive. *At Playa Conchal, you* can get an hour long massage for $35!

Relax, listen to the sound of the waves and have a nice cold pipa fria afterwards!

7. SURFING

People from all over the world come to Costa Rica just to surf because the waves here are some of the best in Latin America. Some of the best beaches for surfing are Pavones, Jaco, Santa Teresa, Playa Hermosa, Playa Cocles, Playa Matapalo (Osa Peninsula), Playa Negra, Playa Guiones, Playa Avellanas, Playa Tamarindo and Playa Grande but this is just a small sampling of the huge number of great surfing beaches here.

There are plenty of surf camps and surf vacations if you want to dedicate more than one day to learn or you can sign up for a one day lesson. A 2 hour group surf lessons costs around $55 or you can rent a board for as little as $12 a day. So if you're visiting any surf town, it's one of the best things to do in Costa Rica you can't miss!

8. CANYONING

Canyoning (rappelling down waterfalls) is an incredible adventure activity in Costa Rica. It might be a bit too much for the ones with acrophobia but the surge of adrenaline flowing through your body takes over and all sense of fear is lost.

Not only is it an adventure of a lifetime but you get to jump down right into the heart of a beautiful Costa Rican forest. It's more exciting than ziplining in my opinion and it's one of our favorite things to do in Costa Rica.

Canyoning is really popular in the La Fortuna/Arenal area as well as outside Playa Hermosa by Jaco. Our favorite is Pure Trek in Arenal, the first waterfall they take you to is nearly 200 feet tall!

9. BEACH HOP

The coasts of Costa Rica are just full of gorgeous beaches and you can find beaches of all characteristics: white sand, dark sand, turquoise waters, clear waters, etc. So when you're at the coast, definitely go beach hopping whether it's by boat or

>TOURIST

foot, it's easily one of the cheapest and best things to do in Costa Rica!

The best part is that no beach is ever so full that you can't find a spot to lay down and if you explore a bit, you may even have a beach all to yourself. And all beaches are public by law so it's one of the best cheap activities to do in Costa Rica.

10. EAT A COPO (OR A CHURCHILL IN PUNTARENAS)

A copo is a Costa Rican shaved ice treat that you can get on nearly every beach. It's shaved ice with kola syrup, powdered milk and condensed milk. Some versions called the churchill are more intense with ice cream and fruit added on top.

Puntarenas is famous for churchills so the best place to get one is there. You can't get a more local dessert than that and it's a yummy way to beat the heat!

11. VISIT THE FIESTAS CIVICAS

There are 9 national holidays in Costa Rica with several more observances, anniversaries and celebrations. Costa Ricans do love a good party and they know how to party hard! For this reason, you can find fiestas civicas, or the local parties all year long. In these parties, they have rides, games, food and bull

The most popular festivities are the Palmares Fiestas, Zapote Fiestas and Puntarenas Carnaval. Thousands of people come to these celebrations from all over Central America every year. Some are religious holidays, some are just a reason to have a good time.

Bull riding is incredibly famous in Costa Rica and they do it all year long with special events during Christmas. For just $10-15, you can hop into the stadium with other daring locals and get chased around by a bull! For those who want to experience local culture, this is one of the best things to do in Costa Rica.

These fiestas are held all year long throughout the country and you will see signs for them in town. The most common months are December, July and February.

12. ISLA TORTUGA CRUISE

The Gulf of Nicoya is home to several beautiful islands in Costa Rica and you can take a day trip to Isla Tortuga, which has a stunning white sand beach. Cruise 1.5 hours through the gulf for spectacular views, relax on the island for 5 hours and boat back at sunset.

This is an excellent day excursion from San Jose and Jaco and a great activity for families. You can go snorkeling, kayaking, jet skiing, swimming and hiking on the island. If you want to do this tour, we have a $10 discount. Check our post on the Tortuga Island day tour here to get the discount.

13. ROAD TRIP THE CENTRAL VALLEY

The landscapes in Costa Rica are simply breathtaking and you can see views just like this driving through the Central Valley. Go off the map and explore the outskirts of big cities and beach towns to experience something authentic and natural.

We drove through Zarcero, Sarchi, Grecia and San Ramon and it was a fantastic way to see small town life, taste local goods and experience a less touristic area in Costa Rica.

14. COMBINATION ADVENTURE TOUR IN RINCON DE LA VIEJA

Combo adventure tours are also another one of our favorite things to do in Guanacaste. We love Guachipelin which consists of ziplining, horseback riding, lunch, river tubing, hot springs and mud baths. It's an awesome adventure in Costa Rica that allows you to experience the best of the volcano and dry tropical forest.

>TOURIST

There are different variations but for an action packed day, a combo tour will fill your need for adventure! Many adventure parks offer combination packages or you can customize your own.

Combination tours cost around $90 and includes lunch, such a great value! If you need transportation, tour companies charge around $140-150.

15. WATERSLIDE IN THE MIDDLE OF THE JUNGLE

Ever wanted to experience the jungle a different way? Waterslide through it at Buena Vista Combo Tour in Guanacaste! This slide is fast as you zip 400 meters through the jungle. I only went twice instead of three times because it was too intense for me!

The water slide is part of a combination tour which also includes horseback riding, ziplining, mud baths and hot springs. It's $98 for the adrenaline tour or $90 for the normal tour.

16. VISIT FINCA TO SEE THE STONE SPHERES

Down in the Osa Peninsula is Finca 6, a designated UENSCO World Heritage Site and museum dedicated to the stone spheres of Costa Rica. The purpose of the spheres have not yet been determined and have been one of the biggest mysteries in Costa Rican history.

This is a great off the beaten path activity near Sierpe and incredibly interesting. It's also an excellent cheap activity in Costa Rica as the entrance fee to the museum is only $6 for adults and $4 for students. You will need your own transportation or you can book a tour which includes transportation and a bilingual guide.

17. STAND UP PADDLE BOARD IN THE OCEAN

Stand up paddle boarding is becoming more popular in Costa Rica and you can rent a board and go on your own or take a class.

>TOURIST

If you're not much of a surfer but still want to get out in the water, SUP is one way to go. It's a good workout for your whole body and a fun way to enjoy the ocean. Some of the best spots are at Playa Manta, Playa Panama and Playa Platanares for their very calm waters.

A board rental varies in cost whether you rent from a company or a hotel. A lesson in Playas del Coco costs $30 for 1 hour.

18. VISIT CATARATA LLANOS DE CORTES

This is one of the best waterfalls in Guanacaste, the stunning Catarata Llanos de Cortes. It's one of our favorite things to do in Liberia, Costa Rica since it's only 20 minutes from the city and the best way to cool off on a hot day.

This small but powerful waterfall has plenty to enjoy besides the water. You can climb up the rocks and sit under the water when it's dry season or you can hike to the top to the waterfall.

Here is our guide to visiting Catarata Llanos de Cortes including our favorite secret spots around the waterfall.

19. VISIT CATARATA DEL TORO

Here's one for the bucket list – the tallest waterfall in Costa Rica! Catarata del Toro is a stunning 270 foot waterfall in an extinct volcano crater hidden in the Central Valley.

You can stop by if you're driving from San Jose to La Fortuna or even stay the night as the private reserve has cabinas. The path down to the waterfall has many steps but it's completely worth it when you get to the bottom! For more information, check out our post on Catarata del Toro.

20. SEE TURTLES AT OSTIONAL WILDLIFE REFUGE

Costa Rica is famous for their huge masses of sea turtles coming to lay their eggs (arribadas). On both

>TOURIST

coasts you can see mother turtles nesting and baby turtles hatching. For animal lovers, this is one of the best wildlife things to do in Costa Rica.

Ostional Wildlife *Refuge* is famous for the mass arrival of Olive Ridley sea turtles with hundreds of thousands of them coming to shore every year. There are many volunteer programs available if you want to do some charity work and help Costa Rica protect their beloved turtles. It's an experience that will make you appreciate nature even more.

You must hire a local guide if you want to enter the refuge or you can walk on the beach outside the refuge without a guide. The best time to go to Ostional WIldlife Refuge is July – December and is one of the best things to do in November as that is usually when the biggest arribadas occur.

21. VISIT THE JAGUAR RESCUE CENTER IN PUERTO VIEJO

If you want to learn more about the wildlife of Costa Rica, the Jaguar Rescue Center is one of the best places to do so. It is a rescue center in Puerto

Viejo de Talamanca that takes in injured animals, rehabilitates them and releases them back to the wild.

They offer guided tours of the center so you can learn about how they are working to help animals such as monkeys, anteaters, sloths and various birds. It's very interesting and the center does great work when it comes to conservation and educating the public on how to interact with wildlife.

22. GO FISHING

Costa Rica is one of the best countries for <u>fishing</u> with healthy waters and knowledgeable locals. Sport fishing in Costa Rica is purely catch and release and you can catch fish like marlin, rooster fish and sail fish.

If you go in shore fishing and catch tuna snapper or mahi mahi, you can keep it. Many restaurants will cook the fish for you too which is nic.

Best places to go fishing in Costa Rica are Playa Flamingo, Tamarindo, Coco, Manuel Antonio, Playa Herradura, Mal Pais, Puntarenas and Drake Bay.

>TOURIST

23. WALK THROUGH SAN JOSE

San Jose really isn't as terrible as people make it out to be. As the capital city, there's a good handful of historical landmarks and it's a good way to get a glimpse of the Costa Rican city life. There are some great cultural things to do in San Jose, Costa Rica as it is the biggest city and where most of the Costa Ricans work. We recommend walking through downtown San Jose to get a feel of how the city is.

Usually 1 or 2 days in San Jose is a good amount of time to explore the city, visit some museums and get a taste of Tico city life. You can even choose San Jose as your home base if you don't want to move around too much in Costa Rica or are limited on time as there are many fun day trips from San Jose.

Go to the south of San Jose to a place called Perez Zeledon and visit Las Cataratas de Nauyaca (Nauyaca Waterfalls) and enjoy beautifull panoramic ambience.

Also visit the Perez Zeledon's Park rest a while if you walked a lot and if you are hungry eat at Cafeteria Tapioca located besides Marisqueria Don Beto, road to the Hopital, there they offer delisious gourmet food and tipical food.

24. KAYAK TORTUGUERO NATIONAL PARK

Tortuguero National Park, or the "Amazon of Costa Rica" is a place like no other in the country. It's famous for turtle nestings and the canals which make up the national park. The national park and town are also boat access only so it's quite an adventure to get there! Once in Tortuguero, you can take boat rides through the national park to see wildlife but our favorite way is to go by kayak.

Kayaking allows you to go to areas that motored boats can't go and you don't disturb the wildlife as much so you can get very close. See toucans, macaws, turtles, monkeys, anteaters and all sorts of wildlife as you glide quietly on the water, surrounded by lush jungle with no one around. This is one of our favorite things to do in Costa Rica because we saw so many animals super close!

Want to visit the national park? Check our Tortugero National Park guide. It is on the Caribbean side so the best time of the year to visit is September and October as it is drier and it's the peak time for turtle nestings.

>TOURIST

25. EXPLORE ARENAL VOLCANO NATIONAL PARK

Arenal Volcano National Park is one of the top three most visited national parks in Costa Rica and is the best place for those who want to see a "cone" shaped volcano. Arenal Volcano erupted back in 1968, leaving a wave of destruction and visitors can hike through the remaining lava beds for beautiful views of the volcano and Lake Arenal.

This is an especially good national park for first timers since it's easy to get to and the trails aren't too tough or long. It's open every day from 8 AM to 4 PM and costs $15 for foreigners. If you walk the Coladas trail, you will reach a viewpoint to see Lake Arenal and the volcano. Visiting Arenal Volcano is a must when in La Fortuna!

26. RIDE A TRAM THROUGH THE RAINFOREST

There are a few trams in Costa Rica that take you through the forest up to stunning views. For those who aren't big hikers or can't do a lot of strenuous movements, the tram is the best way to experience the tropical jungle.

Along the way, it's possible to see various birds, monkeys and other wildlife and it's great to go with a guide who can point out the different plants and flowers you see. And always, at the top is a great view!

Sky Tram at Arenal and Monteverde are excellent ones and Rainforest Adventures Atlantico has a great one on the Caribbean side. Rainforest Adventures also has one outside of Jaco.

27. WHITE WATER RAFT RIO PACUARE

For a full day of fun and adventure, white water rafting at the Rio Pacuare packs all that and more. Raft through class 3 and 4 rapids in the canyons of Costa Rica, bathe in the cool fresh waters and experience a trip of a lifetime.

This is my favorite tour I've ever done in Costa Rica and there are also multi-day white water rafting trips for the more adventurous ones. You can even go

>TOURIST

white water as a way to get around Costa Rica as many companies pick up in San Jose and drop off in La Fortuna or Puerto Viejo! This is definitely one of the top adventure activities in Costa Rica.

If you want to do the tour, we have a Rio Pacuare white water rafting discount to save 10%!

28. GO ON A WATERFALL TOUR

Costa Rica has spectacular waterfalls all throughout the country thanks to the many volcanoes, rivers and valleys. Although you can visit many waterfalls on your own since, there are some waterfalls that are not easily accessible or well known so it's best to go on a tour to see those ones.

We did a waterfall tour in Jaco which was simply amazing. We climbed through the virgin Costa Rican forest up 7 waterfalls, jumping off a few and standing under more. We lived in Jaco for 6 months and would have never known about these waterfalls if we didn't go on the tour!

There are several companies that operate waterfall tours like this one in the Central Pacific. We went with Costa Rica Waterfalls Tours for the one in Jaco and they also operate another tour that goes to really tall waterfalls. In Manuel Antonio, Paddle 9 operates waterfall tours and in Uvita, Rancho Di'Andrew runs waterfalls tours.

29. SEE MONKEYS AND SLOTHS AT MANUEL ANTONIO NATIONAL PARK

Monkeys are always seen at Manuel Antonio National Park so if you want to see monkeys in Costa Rica, Manuel Antonio is one of the best places! You can see three types of monkeys: howler, white face and squirrel.

Other wildlife you can see at Manuel Antonio are toucans, Jesus Christ lizards, raccoons and agoutis. Manuel Antonio National Park is one of the most popular for wildlife because it has simple trails, beautiful beaches and easy accessibility. You don't necessarily need to take a guided hike since the wildlife is quite abundant and easy to spot.

\>TOURIST

30. VISIT A VOLCANO

Costa Rica has a handful of volcanoes and several of them are active such as Arenal, Poas, Turrialba and Rincon de la Vieja. Though you can't hike up to the summit of most volcanoes (it's too dangerous), you can get pretty close.

You can get up to the entrance of Turrialba Volcano National Park for crazy views like this one, you can go all the way up to the crater of Irazu Volcano and hike around the base of Rincon de la Vieja. Poas Volcano National Park is currently indefinitely closed as of 2017 due to extreme volcanic activity.

31. EXPLORE CAVES AT BARRA HONDA NATIONAL PARK

The Nicoya Peninsula is home to some of Costa Rica's most beautiful natural attractions and one of them are the caves. Explore the limestone caves of Costa Rica at Barra Honda National Park, some up to 250 meters deep. Interesting rock formations and stalagmites can be found with columns that look like various shapes in everyday life.

This is probably one of the most unusual things to do in Costa Rica since most people think of jungle and beaches but it is absolutely fascinating. You have to go with a national park guide and the tour is all day. It costs around $75 with transportation.

If you're not interested in the caves, you can visit the national park on your own to hike and see the view points. They also operate tours to see bats since many of them live in the caves and you can't see that in any other part of the country!

32. SEE RIO CELESTE

One of Costa Rica's most magical places is Rio Celeste, a sky blue river in Tenorio Volcano National Park. This bright blue river is stunning and it's even more beautiful in person. It's hard to believe the water is that blue but it really is!

You can hike through Tenorio Volcano National Park along the river to see the waterfall and different parts of the river including the union of the two rivers which creates the blue color. You'll be in awe of this

>TOURIST

spectacular natural landmark when you see for yourself just how blue the water is!

Read our guide to visiting Rio Celeste for more information on how to best experience one of the top sights in Costa Rica.

33. WILDLIFE WATCHING SAFARI FLOAT

One of my all time favorite tours is the river safari float from La Fortuna. We went to a beautiful river in the Cano Negro Wildlife Refuge, which is one of the best places in Costa Rica to see wildlife.

There are two safari floats from La Fortuna: Penas Blancas, the most common one and Rio Frio which is only operated by one tour company, Jacamar Naturalist Tours. Both are wonderful though the Rio Frio is more special as you will be the only boat on the river. And since safari floats are on rafts with paddles, not motors, you can get much closer to the wildlife without disturbing them.

Get 10-15% off the La Fortuna safari float tours here!

34. GO ON A COFFEE TOUR

Costa Rica grows some of the best coffee in the world and if you're a coffee lover, you'll want to take a tour of a coffee plantation to find out why it's so darn good!

It's an incredibly educational and enlightening experience as you learn how a cherry gets from the plant into your cup. Plus you get to sample delicious coffee at the end and purchase coffee and souvenirs.

Our favorite coffee tour is Doka but there are many others. Finca Rosa Blanca is another one of our favorites, it's a working hotel with an auto sustainable coffee plantation and you can go on a coffee tour and tasting to learn about how the grow and process their organic coffee. Since coffee grows best in higher altitudes, the best places for coffee tours are San Jose, Heredia, Turrialba and Monteverde.

35. SEE THE CROCODILES AT RIO TARCOLES

The Rio Tarcoles is famous for one main reason: their crocodiles. As you walk across the bridge and look down, you can see up to 10 or 15 giant crocodiles laying around just a few meters below you.

The bridge is in the town of Tarcoles, a little bit before Jacoand it's worth stopping to see the giant crocodiles.

36. GO ON A CHOCOLATE TOUR

In the past several years, Costa Rica has seen a resurgence in their chocolate production. Cacao grows very well in the tropical climate and you can take tours to see how they grow and process cacao to make chocolate.

The best places to take a chocolate tour is Puerto Viejo and La Fortuna. We did a chocolate tour with the BriBri indigenous community outside Puerto Viejo which was fascinating since chocolate plays such an important part in their culture. We also did one with Rainforest Chocolate Tour in La Fortuna which was really fun and informative.

37. SEE THE WHALE'S TAIL AT MARINO BALLENA NATIONAL PARK

Costa Rica is full of stunning natural treasures and Marino Ballena National Park is one of them. Inside the park, there is a section where two beaches come together so in low tide, it looks like a whale's tail!

If you go in high tide, the water covers the whole thing and you can't see it. The Whale's Tail is appropriately named as that area is one of the best places in Costa Rica to see humpback whales!

38. EAT A CHIFRIJO

Looking for a classic Costa Rican dish? Order a chifrijo! It is a mix of rice, beans, pico de gallo and chicharrones (fried pork). It comes with chips and best eaten at the bar with a beer. There's nothing more Costa Rican than a chifrijo and Imperial beer!

You can find it on the menu at most Costa Rican bars and sodas but it may be under another name. If you don't see it, just ask. Costa Ricans love this dish!

>TOURIST

39. EAT RICE AND BEANS

If you go to the Caribbean side of Costa Rica, you'll be surprised to see that the culture, food and people are completely different. This is one of the must things to do in Costa Rica so you can experience the varying cultures between the Caribbean and the rest of the country.

Instead of gallo pinto, they eat rice and beans which has coconut milk in it. Their culture is highly influenced by the nearby Caribbean islands so you'll find plenty of jerk chicken and other yummy dishes.

Our favorite place to get rice and beans in Puerto Viejo is Soda Lidia's Place. Get the chicken and add some hot sauce, it's heavenly!

40. ENJOY THE HOT SPRINGS IN ARENAL

Arenal has some of the best hot springs in the country with the Tabacon river supplying natural hot water to the springs. Some hotels have their own private hot springs or you can go to free access part of the river where the locals go.

Tabacon, Baldi and Titoku are just a few places you can bathe in and enjoy the thermal waters. Baldi is best for kids, Tabacon is ideal for couples and Paraiso and Ecotermales are great for those who don't want to be around a lot of people. If you're visiting La Fortuna, going to the hot springs is a must! You can read more about the best hot springs in Arenal in this post.

41. GO WHALE WATCHING

Costa Rica has the longest humpback whale watching season in the world so your chances are pretty good to see these magnificent creatures. If you love whales, the ocean or wildlife, this is a must do activity in Costa Rica.

>TOURIST

The best places for whale watching is down in Uvita, Drake Bay and Gulf of Papagayo. The best months are August and September but in Uvita, you have a chance to see them from July – November and January – April since both northern and southern humpback whales pass through. We have seen humpback and pilot whales in the Gulf of Papagayo and gone on a humpback whale watching tour in Uvita.

42. GET A PIPA FRIA

You'll see signs for pipa fria at every beach town and you definitely want to try one. It's cold coconut water and is oh so delicious on a hot day!

I love watching the vendors hack off the top with a huge machete (they do it with such precision), hand you the pipa and keep hacking other coconuts. They are coconut experts!

You can find vendors at nearly every beach and it costs around 500 colones a pipa fria.

43. GO BIRD WATCHING

With over 800 species of birds living in Costa Rica, any bird lover will be in paradise. Snap photos of hummingbirds, toucans, macaws, parrots and other gorgeous tropical birds all throughout the country.

Wildlife and bird lovers have to put a bird watching tour on their "things to do in Costa Rica' list. Many hotels and tour companies offer bird watching tours, especially down in the Osa Peninsula, Tortuguero, Puerto Viejo, Arenal and Monteverde as those are the top places to see a diverse amount of birds. They usually start around 530 AM since birds are more active in the morning and take you either to an observation platform or hiking around the forest.

44. PLAY WITH PUPPIES AT TERRITORIO DE ZAGUATES

Territorio de Zagutes is the biggest no kill shelter in the world. They have anywhere from 700-900 dogs at one time living on their insanely large property up in the hills outside of Heredia and they host open

>TOURIST

walks every month for visitors to play, run and enjoy the company of hundreds of dogs.

The couple that runs the shelter works incredibly hard to give these street dogs the care and love they deserve including health check ups, vaccinations and getting them adopted. You can adopt a dog or simply donate as they don't charge an entrance fee for visiting doggie paradise.

Read our guide to visiting Territorio de Zaguates for more information.

45. GO ON A NIGHT WALK

The jungle changes drastically when the sun goes down and the best way to experience it is to go for a guided night walk (you don't want to be wandering the forest on your own!). Guides will point out creatures that are only seen in the dark such as insects, spiders, frogs, snakes and more.

We've done several night walks in Costa Rica. In Arenal, we did a night walk with Jacamar (get 10% off this tour). In Osa Peninsula we did a night walk at Leona station with La Leona Eco-Lodge, in Braulio

Carrillo we did a night walk with Rainforest Adventures and in Monteverde we did one at Finca Santa Maria. For night walks in Manuel Antonio, we recommend Si Como No Hotel which has a private reserve. We also did one in Bijagua at Tapir Valley.

46. WATCH A FUTBOL GAME AT THE NATIONAL STADIUM IN LA SABANA

Vamos Ticos!

Futbol is a huge passion of all Costa Ricans and there are games held in the stadium year round. Cheer for the local teams and experience one of the country's favorite past times.

Also the Costa Rican national team goalie Keylor Navas plays for the Real Madrid so if you think Costa Rica doesn't have good players, you're definitely wrong on that part! La Sabana in San Jose is their biggest stadium but they also have stadiums in Heredia, Puntarenas, Alajuela, Limon and Cartago.

We watched the Panama vs Costa Rica game in La Sabana (qualifiers for World Cup) and it was really fun to see all the Ticos cheering and going crazy!

>TOURIST

47. TRY COSTA RICAN LOCAL AND CRAFT BEER

Costa Rica has a few locals beers to try, Pilsen and Imperial are the most popular. Head to the bar to have a beer and you'll also get a great glimpse into Tico life since beer is heavily ingrained in their culture. All bars in Costa Rica offer some sort of happy hour, some places even have happy hour all day!

Costa Rican craft beer is getting really popular and many high end restaurants and bars offer craft beer. Witch's Rock Surf Camp in Tamarindo has a new bar with 18 different craft beers and in San Jose, you can take a beer tour to the Ceverceria. Micro-breweries are popping up all throughout the country and in pretty much every touristic destination.

48. HIKE CORCOVADO NATIONAL PARK

As one of the most biologically diverse places on earth, Corcovado National Park is an absolute must for hikers and wildlife lovers. It's such a unique place in Costa Rica, you feel like it's a different world with the sheer amount of wildlife around. Corcovado National Park is in the Osa Peninsula, which holds around 6% of the world's biodiversity.

You can do a one day hiking trip to the ranger stations such as La Leona, San Pedrillo and Sirena but the ultimate way to experience the national park is to do an overnight hiking trip. The most popular one is from La Leona to Sirena where it's possible to see tapirs, pumas, anteaters and more.

You now have to go with a guide if you want to do the overnight 14 kilometer hike and reserve a spot beforehand. Make sure to pack properly and be prepared for the humidity as this area is incredibly humid. If you want to visit Osa Peninsula where Corcovado National Park is, check our Osa Peninsula guide for more tips on how to visit the national park and get the most of this area.

>TOURIST

49. WALK THE HANGING BRIDGES IN THE MONTEVERDE CLOUD FORESTS

Walking the hanging bridges in Monteverde gives you a great view of the cloud forest as each one goes up higher and higher. You can see lush green forest all around you and even some wildlife if you have a good eye.

Don't worry, these bridges are all very stable and secure and is one of the best ways to take in the beauty of Costa Rica. Many of the adventure parks have their own hanging bridges
like Selvatura and Sky Trek. There is also one hanging bridge inside the Monteverde Cloud Forest Biological Reserve.

50. ENJOY THE PURA VIDA LIFE!

And of all the things to do in Costa Rica, the most important one is to enjoy the pura vida life.

Costa Rica is a country full of love and peace and their people know how to live and enjoy. They'll teach you how to be grateful for what you have and you'll take all those things with you when you go back to your home country. Hopefully your trip here will give you a new perspective on life and to appreciate what is given to you.

>TOURIST

BONUS TIPS

50 THINGS TO KNOW ABOUT PACKING LIGHT FOR TRAVEL

PACK THE RIGHT WAY EVERY TIME

AUTHOR: MANIDIPA BHATTACHARYYA

First Published in 2015 by Dr. Lisa Rusczyk. Copyright 2015. All Rights Reserved. No part of this publication may be reproduced, including scanning and photocopying, or distributed in any form or by any means, electronic or mechanical, or stored in a database or retrieval system without prior written permission from the publisher.

Disclaimer: The publisher has put forth an effort in preparing and arranging this book. The information provided herein by the author is provided "as is". Use this information at your own risk. The publisher is not a licensed doctor. Consult your doctor before engaging in any medical activities. The publisher and author disclaim any liabilities for any loss of profit or commercial or personal damages resulting from the information contained in this book.

Edited by Melanie Howthorne

ABOUT THE AUTHOR

Manidipa Bhattacharyya is a creative writer and editor, with an education in English literature and Linguistics. After working in the IT industry for seven long years she decided to call it quits and follow her heart instead. Manidipa has been ghost writing, editing, proof reading and doing secondary research services for many story tellers and article writers for about three years. She stays in Kolkata, India with her husband and a busy two year old. In her own time Manidipa enjoys travelling, photography and writing flash fiction.

Manidipa believes in travelling light and never carries anything that she couldn't haul herself on a trip. However, travelling with her child changed the scenario. She seemed to carry the entire world with her for the baby on the first two trips. But good sense prevailed and she is again working her way to becoming a light traveler, this time with a kid.

>TOURIST

INTRODUCTION

*He who would travel happily
must travel light.*

-Antoine de Saint-Exupéry

Travel takes you to different places from seas and mountains to deserts and much more. In your travels you get to interact with different people and their cultures. You will, however, enjoy the sights and interact positively with these new people even more, if you are travelling light.

When you travel light your mind can be free from worry about your belongings. You do not have to spend precious vacation time waiting for your luggage to arrive after a long flight. There is be no chance of your bags going missing and the best part is that you need not pay a fee for checked baggage.

People who have mastered this art of packing light will root for you to take only one carry-on, wherever you go. However, many people can find it really hard to pack light. More so if you are travelling with children. Differentiating between "must have" and "just in case" items is the starting point. There will be ample shopping avenues at your destination which are just waiting to be explored.

This book will show you 'packing' in a new 'light' – pun intended – and help you to embrace light packing practices for all of your future travels.

Off to packing!

DEDICATION

I dedicate this book to all the travel buffs that I know, who have given me great insights into the contents of their backpacks.

THE RIGHT TRAVEL GEAR

1. CHOOSE YOUR TRAVEL GEAR CAREFULLY

While selecting your travel gear, pick items that are light weight, durable and most importantly, easy to carry. There are cases with wheels so you can drag them along – these are usually on the heavy side because of the trolley. Alternatively a backpack that you can carry comfortably on your back, or even a duffel bag that you can carry easily by hand or sling across your body are also great options. Whatever you choose, one thing to keep in mind is that the luggage itself should not weigh a ton, this will give you the flexibility to bring along one extra pair of shoes if you so desire.

>TOURIST

2. CARRY THE MINIMUM NUMBER OF BAGS

Selecting light weight luggage is not everything. You need to restrict the number of bags you carry as well. One carry-on size bag is ideal for light travel. Most carriers allow one cabin baggage plus one purse, handbag or camera bag as long as it slides under the seat in front. So technically, you can carry two items of luggage without checking them in.

3. PACK ONE EXTRA BAG

Always pack one extra empty bag along with your essential items. This could be a very light weight duffel bag or even a sturdy tote bag which takes up minimal space. In the event that you end up buying a lot of souvenirs, you already have a handy bag to stuff all that into and do not have to spend time hunting for an appropriate bag.

> *I'm very strict with my packing and have everything in its right place. I never change a rule. I hardly use anything in the hotel room. I wheel my own wardrobe in and that's it.*
>
> Charlie Watts

CLOTHES & ACCESSORIES

4. PLAN AHEAD

Figure out in advance what you plan to do on your trip. That will help you to pick that one dress you need for the occasion. If you are going to attend a wedding then you have to carry formal wear. If not, you can ditch the gown for something lighter that will be comfortable during long walks or on the beach.

5. WEAR THAT JACKET

Remember that wearing items will not add extra luggage for your air travel. So wear that bulky jacket that you plan to carry for your trip. This saves space and can also help keep you warm during the chilly flight.

6. MIX AND MATCH

Carry clothes that can be interchangeably used to reinvent your look. Find one top that goes well with a couple of pairs of pants or skirts. Use tops, shirts and jackets wisely along with other accessories like a scarf or a stole to create a new look.

>TOURIST

7. CHOOSE YOUR FABRIC WISELY

Stuffing clothes in cramped bags definitely takes its toll which results in wrinkles. It is best to carry wrinkle free, synthetic clothes or merino tops. This will eliminate the need for that small iron you usually bring along.

8. DITCH CLOTHES PACK UNDERWEAR

Pack more underwear and socks. These are the things that will give you a fresh feel even if you do not get a chance to wear fresh clothes. Moreover these are easy to wash and can be dried inside the hotel room itself.

9. CHOOSE DARK OVER LIGHT

While picking your clothes choose dark coloured ones. They are easy to colour coordinate and can last longer before needing a wash. Accidental food spills and dirt from the road are less visible on darker clothes.

10. WEAR YOUR JEANS

Take only one pair of Jeans with you, which you should wear on the flight. Remember to pick a pair that can be worn for sightseeing trips and is equally eloquent for dinner. You can add variety by adding light weight cargoes and chinos.

11. CARRY SMART ACCESSORIES

The right accessory can give you a fresh look even with the same old dress. An intelligent neck-piece, a couple of bright scarves, stoles or a sarong can be used in a number of ways to add variety to your clothing. These light weight beauties can double up as a nursing cover, a light blanket, beach wear, a modesty cover for visiting places of worship, and also makes for an enthralling game of peek-a-boo.

12. LEARN TO FOLD YOUR GARMENTS

Seasoned travellers all swear by rolling their clothes for compact and wrinkle free packing. Bundle packing, where you roll the clothes around a central object as if tying it up, is also a popular method of compact and wrinkle free packing. Stacking folded clothes one on top of another is a big no-no as it makes creases extreme and they are difficult to get rid of without ironing.

13. WASH YOUR DIRTY LAUNDRY

One of the ways to avoid carrying loads of clothes is to wash the clothes you carry. At some places you might get to use the laundry services or a Laundromat but if you are in a pinch, best solution is to wash them yourself. If that is the plan then carrying quick drying clothes is highly recommended, which most often also happen to be the wrinkle free variety.

14. LEAVE THOSE TOWELS BEHIND

Regular towels take up a lot of space, are heavy and take ages to dry out. If you are staying at hotels they will provide you with towels anyway. If you are travelling to a remote place, where the availability of towels look doubtful, carry a light weight travel towel of viscose material to do the job.

15. USE A COMPRESSION BAG

Compression bags are getting lots of recommendation now days from regular travellers. These are useful for saving space in your luggage when you have to pack bulky dresses. While packing for the return trip, get help from the hotel staff to arrange a vacuum cleaner.

FOOTWEAR

16. PUT ON YOUR HIKING BOOTS

If you have plans to go hiking or trekking during your trip, you will need those bulky hiking boots. The best way to carry them is to wear them on flight to save space and luggage weight. You can remove the boots once inside and be comfortable in your socks.

17. PICKING THE RIGHT SHOES

Shoes are often the bulkiest items, along with being the dainty if you are a female. They need care and take up a lot of space in your luggage. It is advisable therefore to pick shoes very carefully. If you plan to do a lot of walking and site seeing, then wearing a pair of comfortable walking shoes are a must. For more formal occasions you can carry durable, light weight flats which will not take up much space.

18. STUFF SHOES

If you happen to pack a pair of shoes, ensure you utilize their hollow insides. Tuck small items like rolled up socks or belts to save space. They will also be easy to find.

>TOURIST

TOILETRIES

19. STASHING TOILETRIES

Carry only absolute necessities. Airline rules dictate that for one carry-on bag, liquids and gels must be in 3.4 ounce (100ml) bottles or less, and must be packed in a one quart zip-lock bag. If you are planning to stay in a hotel, the basic things will be provided for you. It's best is to buy the rest from the local market at your destination.

20. TAKE ALONG TAMPONS

Tampons are a hard to find item in a lot of countries. Figure out how many you need and pack accordingly. For longer stays you can buy them online and have them delivered to where you are staying.

21. GET PAMPERED BEFORE YOU TRAVEL

Some avid travellers suggest getting a pedicure and manicure just the day before travelling. This not only gives you a well kept look, you also save the trouble of packing nail polish. Remember, every little bit of weight reduced adds up.

ELECTRONICS

22. LUGGING ALONG ELECTRONICS

Electronics have a large role to play in our lives today. Most of us cannot imagine our lives away from our phones, laptops or tablets. However while travelling, one must consider the amount of weight these electronics add to our luggage. Thankfully smart phones come along with all the essentials tools like a camera, email access, picture editing tools and more. They are smart to the point of eliminating the need to carry multiple gadgets. Choose a smart phone that suits all your requirements and travel with the world in your palms or pocket.

23. REDUCE THE NUMBER OF CHARGERS

If you do travel with multiple electronic devices, you will have to bear the additional burden of carrying all their chargers too. Check if a single charger can be used for multiple devices. You might also consider investing in a pocket charger. These small devices support multiple devices while keeping you charged on the go.

>TOURIST

24. TRAVEL FRIENDLY APPS

Along with smart phones come numerous apps, which are immensely helpful in our travels. You name it and you have an app for it at hand – take pictures, sharing with friends and family, torch to light dark roads, maps, checking flight/train times, find hotels and many other things. Use these smart alternatives to traditional items like books to eliminate weight and save space.

I get ideas about what's essential when packing my suitcase.

-Diane von Furstenberg

TRAVELLING WITH KIDS

25. BRING ALONG THE STROLLER

Kids might enjoy walking for a while but they soon tire out and a stroller is the just the right thing for them to rest in while you continue your tour. Strollers also double duty as a luggage carrier and shopping bag holder. Remember to pick a light weight, easy to handle brand of stroller. Better yet, find out in advance if you can rent a stroller at your destination.

26. BRING ONLY ENOUGH DIAPERS FOR YOUR TRIP

Diapers take up a lot of space and add to the weight of your luggage. Therefore it is advisable to carry just enough diapers to last through the trip and a few for afterwards, till you buy fresh stock at your destination. Unless of course you are travelling to a really remote area, in which case you have no choice but to carry the load. Otherwise diapers are something you will find pretty easily.

27. TAKE ONLY A COUPLE OF TOYS

Children are easily attracted by new things in their environment. While travelling they will find numerous 'new' objects to scrutinize and play with. Packing just one favorite toy is enough, or if there is no favorite toy leave out all of them in favor of stories or imaginary games.

28. CARRY KID FRIENDLY SNACKS

Create a small snack counter in your bag to store away quick bites for those sudden hunger pangs. Depending on the child's age this could include chocolates, raisins, dry fruits, granola bars or biscuits. Also keep a bottle of water handy for your little one.

>TOURIST

These things do not add much weight and can be adjusted in a handbag or knapsack.

29. GAMES TO CARRY

Create some travel specific, imaginary games if you have slightly grown up children, like spot the attractions. Keep a coloring book and colors handy for in-flight or hotel time. Apps on your smart phone can keep the children engaged with cartoons and story books. Older children are often entertained by games available on phones or tablets. This cuts the weight of luggage down while keeping the kids entertained.

30. LET THE KIDS CARRY THEIR LOAD

A good thing is to start early sharing of responsibilities. Let your child pick a bag of his or her choice and pack it themselves. Keep tabs on what they are stuffing in their bags by asking if they will be using that item on the trip. It could start out being just an entertainment bag initially but with growing years they will learn to sort the useful from the superfluous. Children as little as four can maneuver a small trolley suitcase like a pro- their experience in pull along toys credit. If you are worried that you may be pulling it for them, you may want to start with a backpack.

31. DECIDE ON LOCATION FOR CHILDREN TO SLEEP

While on a trip you might not always get a crib at your destination, and carrying one will make life all the more difficult. Instead call ahead to see if there are any cribs or roll out beds for children. You may even put blankets on the floor. Weave them a story about camping and they will gladly sleep without any trouble.

32. GET BABY PRODUCTS DELIVERED AT YOUR DESTINATION

If you are absolutely paranoid about not getting your favourite variety of diaper or brand of baby food, check out online stores like amazon.com for services in your destination city. You can buy things online ahead of your travel and get them delivered to your hotel upon arrival.

33. FEEDING NEEDS OF YOUR INFANTS

If you are travelling with a breastfed infant, you save the trouble of carrying bottles and bottle sanitization kits. For special food, or medications, you may need

>TOURIST

to call ahead to make sure you have a refrigerator where you are staying.

34. FEEDING NEEDS OF YOUR TODDLER

With the progression from infancy to toddler, their dietary requirements too evolve. You will have to pack some snacks for travelling time. Fresh fruits and vegetables can be purchased at your destination. Most of the cities you travel to in whichever part of the world, will have baby food products and formulas, available at the local drug-store or the supermarket.

35. PICKING CLOTHES FOR YOUR BABY

Contrary to popular belief, babies can do without many changes of clothes. At the most pack 2 outfits per day. Pack mix and match type clothes for your little one as well. Pick things which are comfortable to wear and quick to dry.

36. SELECTING SHOES FOR YOUR BABY

Like outfits, kids can make do with two pairs of comfortable shoes. If you can get some water resistant shoes it will be best. To expedite drying wet shoes, you can stuff newspaper in them then wrap them with newspaper and leave them to dry overnight.

37. KEEP ONE CHANGE OF CLOTHES HANDY

Travelling with kids can be tricky. Keep a change of clothes for the kids and mum handy in your purse or tote bag. This takes a bit of space in your hand luggage but comes extremely handy in case there are any accidents or spills.

38. LEAVE BEHIND BABY ACCESSORIES

Baby accessories like their bed, bath tub, car seat, crib etc. should be left at home. Many hotels provide a crib on request, while car seats can be borrowed from friends or rented. Babies can be given a bath in the hotel sink or even in the adult bath tub with a little bit of water. If you bring a few bath toys, they can be used in the bath, pool, and out of water. They can also be sanitized easily in the sink.

39. CARRY A SMALL LOAD OF PLASTIC BAGS

With children around there are chances of a number of soiled clothes and diapers. These plastic bags help to sort the dirt from the clean inside your big bag.

> TOURIST

These are very light weight and come in handy to other carry stuff as well at times.

PACK WITH A PURPOSE

40. PACKING FOR BUSINESS TRIPS

One neutral-colored suit should suffice. It can be paired with different shirts, ties and accessories for different occasions. One pair of black suit pants could be worn with a matching jacket for the office or with a snazzy top for dinner.

41. PACKING FOR A CRUISE

Most cruises have formal dinners, and that formal dress usually takes up a lot of space. However you might find a tuxedo to rent. For women, a short black dress with multiple accessory options will do the trick.

42. PACKING FOR A LONG TRIP OVER DIFFERENT CLIMATES

The secret packing mantra for travel over multiple climates is layering. Layering traps air around your body creating insulation against the cold. The same light t-shirt that is comfortable in a warmer climate can be the innermost layer in a colder climate.

REDUCE SOME MORE WEIGHT

43. LEAVE PRECIOUS THINGS AT HOME

Things that you would hate to lose or get damaged leave them at home. Precious jewelry, expensive gadgets or dresses, could be anything. You will not require these on your trip. Leave them at home and spare the load on your mind.

44. SEND SOUVENIRS BY MAIL

If you have spent all your money on purchasing souvenirs, carrying them back in the same bag that you brought along would be difficult. Either pack everything in another bag and check it in the airport or get everything shipped to your home. Use an international carrier for a secure transit, but this could be more expensive than the checking fees at the airport.

45. AVOID CARRYING BOOKS

Books equal to weight. There are many reading apps which you can download on your smart phone or tab.

> TOURIST

Plus there are gadgets like Kindle and Nook that are thinner and lighter alternatives to your regular book.

CHECK, GET, SET, CHECK AGAIN

46. STRATEGIZE BEFORE PACKING

Create a travel list and prepare all that you think you need to carry along. Keep everything on your bed or floor before packing and then think through once again – do I really need that? Any item that meets this question can be avoided. Remove whatever you don't really need and pack the rest.

47. TEST YOUR LUGGAGE

Once you have fully packed for the trip take a test trip with your luggage. Take your bags and go to town for window shopping for an hour. If you enjoy your hour long trip it is good to go, if not, go home and reduce the load some more. Repeat this test till you hit the right weight.

48. ADD A ROLL OF DUCT TAPE

You might wonder why, when this book has been talking about reducing stuff, we're suddenly asking you to pack something totally unusual. This is because when you have limited supplies, duct tape is immensely helpful for small repairs – a broken bag, leaking zip-lock bag, broken sunglasses, you name it and duct tape can fix it, temporarily.

49. LIST OF ESSENTIAL ITEMS

Even though the emphasis is on packing light, there are things which have to be carried for any trip. Here is our list of essentials:

- Passport/Visa or any other ID

- Any other paper work that might be required on a trip like permits, hotel reservation confirmations etc.

- Medicines – all your prescription medicines and emergency kit, especially if you are travelling with children

- Medical or vaccination records

- Money in foreign currency if travelling to a different country

- Tickets- Email or Message them to your phone

>TOURIST

50. MAKE THE MOST OF YOUR TRIP

Wherever you are going, whatever you hope to do we encourage you to embrace it whole-heartedly. Take in the scenery, the culture and above all, enjoy your time away from home.

> *On a long journey even a straw weighs heavy.*
>
> -Spanish Proverb

>TOURIST

PACKING AND PLANNING TIPS

A Week before Leaving

- Arrange for someone to take care of pets and water plants.
- Email and Print important Documents.
- Get Visa and vaccines if needed.
- Check for travel warnings.
- Stop mail and newspaper.
- Notify Credit Card companies where you are going.
- Passports and photo identification is up to date.
- Pay bills.
- Copy important items and download travel Apps.
- Start collecting small bills for tips.
- Have post office hold mail while you are away.
- Check weather for the week.
- Car inspected, oil is changed, and tires have the correct pressure.
- Check airline luggage restrictions.
- Download Apps needed for your trip.

Right Before Leaving

- Contact bank and credit cards to tell them your location.
- Clean out refrigerator.
- Empty garbage cans.
- Lock windows.
- Make sure you have the proper identification with you.
- Bring cash for tips.
- Remember travel documents.
- Lock door behind you.
- Remember wallet.
- Unplug items in house and pack chargers.
- Change your thermostat settings.
- Charge electronics, and prepare camera memory cards.

>TOURIST

READ OTHER GREATER THAN A TOURIST BOOKS

Greater Than a Tourist- Geneva Switzerland: 50 Travel Tips from a Local by Amalia Kartika

Greater Than a Tourist- St. Croix US Birgin Islands USA: 50 Travel Tips from a Local by Tracy Birdsall

Greater Than a Tourist- San Juan Puerto Rico: 50 Travel Tips from a Local by Melissa Tait

Greater Than a Tourist – Lake George Area New York USA: 50 Travel Tips from a Local by Janine Hirschklau

Greater Than a Tourist – Monterey California United States: 50 Travel Tips from a Local by Katie Begley

Greater Than a Tourist – Chanai Crete Greece: 50 Travel Tips from a Local by Dimitra Papagrigoraki

Greater Than a Tourist – The Garden Route Western Cape Province South Africa: 50 Travel Tips from a Local by Li-Anne McGregor van Aardt

Greater Than a Tourist – Sevilla Andalusia Spain: 50 Travel Tips from a Local by Gabi Gazon

Children's Book: *Charlie the Cavalier Travels the World* by Lisa Rusczyk

> TOURIST

Visit *Greater Than a Tourist* for Free Travel Tips
http://GreaterThanATourist.com

Sign up for the *Greater Than a Tourist* Newsletter for discount days, new books, and travel information:
http://eepurl.com/cxspyf

Follow us on Facebook for tips, images, and ideas:
https://www.facebook.com/GreaterThanATourist

Follow us on Pinterest for travel tips and ideas:
http://pinterest.com/GreaterThanATourist

Follow us on Instagram for beautiful travel images:
http://Instagram.com/GreaterThanATourist

Follow *Greater Than a Tourist* on Amazon.

At *Greater Than a Tourist*, we love to share travel tips with you. How did we do? What guidance do you have for how we can give you better advice for your next trip? Please send your feedback to GreaterThanaTourist@gmail.com as we continue to improve the series. We appreciate your constructive feedback. Thank you.

METRIC CONVERSIONS

TEMPERATURE

110° F — — 40° C
100° F —
90° F — — 30° C
80° F —
70° F — — 20° C
60° F —
50° F — — 10° C
40° F —
32° F — — 0° C
20° F —
10° F — — -10° C
0° F —
-10° F — — -18° C
-20° F — — -30° C

To convert F to C:
Subtract 32, and then multiply by 5/9 or .5555.

To Convert C to F:
Multiply by 1.8 and then add 32.

32F = 0C

LIQUID VOLUME

To Convert:	Multiply by
U.S. Gallons to Liters	3.8
U.S. Liters to Gallons	26
Imperial Gallons to U.S. Gallons	1.2
Imperial Gallons to Liters	4.55
Liters to Imperial Gallons	22

1 Liter = .26 U.S. Gallon
1 U.S. Gallon = 3.8 Liters

DISTANCE

To convert	Multiply by
Inches to Centimeters	2.54
Centimeters to Inches	39
Feet to Meters	.3
Meters to Feet	3.28
Yards to Meters	91
Meters to Yards	1.09
Miles to Kilometers	1.61
Kilometers to Miles	.62

1 Mile = 1.6 km
1 km = .62 Miles

WEIGHT

1 Ounce = .28 Grams
1 Pound = .4555 Kilograms
1 Gram = .04 Ounce
1 Kilogram = 2.2 Pounds

>TOURIST

TRAVEL QUESTIONS

- Do you bring presents home to family or friends after a vacation?
- Do you get motion sick?
- Do you have a favorite billboard?
- Do you know what to do if there is a flat tire?
- Do you like a sun roof open?
- Do you like to eat in the car?
- Do you like to wear sun glasses in the car?
- Do you like toppings on your ice cream?
- Do you use public bathrooms?
- Did you bring your cell phone and does it have power?
- Do you have a form of identification with you?
- Have you ever been pulled over by a cop?
- Have you ever given money to a stranger on a road trip?
- Have you ever taken a road trip with animals?
- Have you ever went on a vacation alone?
- Have you ever run out of gas?

- If you could move to any place in the world, where would it be?
- If you could travel anywhere in the world, where would you travel?
- If you could travel in any vehicle, which one would it be?
- If you had three things to wish for from a magic genie, what would they be?
- If you have a driver's license, how many times did it take you to pass the test?
- What are you the most afraid of on vacation?
- What do you want to get away from the most when you are on vacation?
- What foods smells bad to you?
- What item do you bring on ever trip with you away from home?
- What makes you sleepy?
- What song would you love to hear on the radio when you're cruising on the highway?
- What travel job would you want the least?
- What will you miss most while you are away from home?
- What is something you always wanted to try?

>TOURIST

- What is the best road side attraction that you ever saw?
- What is the farthest distance you ever biked?
- What is the farthest distance you ever walked?
- What is the weirdest thing you needed to buy while on vacation?
- What is your favorite candy?
- What is your favorite color car?
- What is your favorite family vacation?
- What is your favorite food?
- What is your favorite gas station drink or food?
- What is your favorite license plate design?
- What is your favorite restaurant?
- What is your favorite smell?
- What is your favorite song?
- What is your favorite sound that nature makes?
- What is your favorite thing to bring home from a vacation?
- What is your favorite vacation with friends?
- What is your favorite way to relax?

- Where is the farthest place you ever traveled in a car?
- Where is the farthest place you ever went North, South, East and West?
- Where is your favorite place in the world?
- Who is your favorite singer?
- Who taught you how to drive?
- Who will you miss the most while you are away?
- Who if the first person you will contact when you get to your destination?
- Who brought you on your first vacation?
- Who likes to travel the most in your life?
- Would you rather be hot or cold?
- Would you rather drive above, below, or at the speed limited?
- Would you rather drive on a highway or a back road?
- Would you rather go on a train or a boat?
- Would you rather go to the beach or the woods?

>TOURIST

TRAVEL BUCKET LIST

1.

2.

3.

4.

5.

6.

7.

8.

9.

10.

Made in the USA
Las Vegas, NV
26 March 2023